Java 23 New Features Simplified

Vijay SRJ

Contents

Introduction

Java is growing day by day.

Until Java 8 the pace at which new features were introduced in Java was gradual.

And then Java 8 happened. Streams and Lambdas arrived along with a lot of other features. And since then, every 6 months Java is coming up with new features.

These are targeted to improve developer productivity, the language's performance, security and maintainability.

Java introduces changes in a structured way. New features are introduced as preview features and the experimental ones as incubator modules. They are called JEPs (JDK Enhancement Proposals) and have a unique number associated with them.

The preview features mostly go through three reviews (first preview, second preview and third preview) and finally get accepted as a permanent feature. The incubator features are, as already mentioned experimental features and once stable will go through the preview process and finally get accepted into the language permanently.

Java 23 released 12 enhancements of which 8 are in preview feature and 1 in incubator mode. Of the 12, 4 of them are language improvements, 5 are library changes, 1 change related to performance, 1 related to tooling and 1 related to stewardship

With Java 23 you can,

- Use primitive types like int, float in instanceof, switch and pattern matching

- Create custom intermediate operations in Streams

- Create a main method without using "public static" keyword and not even define it inside a class.

- Perform concurrency in a structured way using Structured Concurrency

- Create thread level constants using Scoped Values

- Allow statements before super() and this() methods in constructors

- Import an entire module in your class using "import module" keyword

    And few more ...

A lot of them are in preview mode so to use it you need to set preview feature flag and is advisable not to use in production until Java finalizes them in the future releases.

Here is the entire list of JEPs in Java 23 under different categories:

Language improvements:

455:    Primitive Types in Patterns, instanceof, and switch (Preview)

476:    Module Import Declarations (Preview)

477:    Implicitly Declared Classes and Instance Main Methods (Third Preview)

482:    Flexible Constructor Bodies (Second Preview)

Libraries:

466:    Class-File API (Second Preview)

469:    Vector API (Eighth Incubator)

473:    Stream Gatherers (Second Preview)

480:    Structured Concurrency (Third Preview)

481:    Scoped Values (Third Preview)

Performance:

474:    ZGC: Generational Mode by Default

Tooling:

467:    Markdown Documentation Comments

Stewardship

471:    Deprecate the Memory-Access Methods in sun.misc.Unsafe for Removal

Primitive Types in Patterns, Instanceof and Switch

Pattern matching for switch

The switch statement in Java has gone through a rapid evolution since Java 7.

Until Java 7, you could compare only integers.

Then Java 8 allowed you to compare strings and enums.

And Java 12 allowed you to return values from a switch block and have multiple values in a case label.

Java 17 came up with a new feature altogether,

You could compare "types" instead of actual "values" in switch statement.

```java
public String check(Object o){

    return switch(o){

        case Integer i -> "it is an integer";
        case String s -> "it is a string";
        case Car c -> "it us a user defined car object";
        default -> " I have no idea what this is";

    };

}
```

Notice the case labels.

They are defined using the data type followed by a variable name, eg : Integer i.

So, if the passed value is an integer this label will get matched and the value will be assigned to the variable i which you can use inside the case block.

This is called **pattern matching**.

But this had a limitation,

You cannot use primitive types like int, byte, char etc in this "pattern matching".

You can use only reference types like Integer, String and classes defined by the developer (like Car in the above example).

That is now possible in Java 23.

So, the below code is valid now:

```
public String check(Object o){

    return switch(o){

        case int i -> "it is an integer";
        case char c -> "it is a character";

        default -> " i have no idea what this is";

    };

}
```

You can also add guards using 'when' keyword just like for reference types:

```
public String check(Object o){

    return switch(o){
        case int i when i < 100 -> "it is a small integer";
        case int i -> "it is a large integer";
        case char c -> "it is a character";

        default -> " i have no idea what this is";

    };}
```

Pattern matching for instanceof

instanceof operator is used to check if the given value belongs to a particular instance. You often do it along with casting operation.

For example:

```
Object add(Object obj) {

    if (obj instanceof Integer) {

        Integer value = (Integer) obj;

        return value + value;
    }

    if (obj instanceof String) {

        String value = (String) obj;
```

```
        return value + value;
    }
    return null;

}
```

Java introduced pattern matching for instanceof operation and you can avoid the casting now like below:

```
Object addWithPatternMatching(Object obj) {

    if (obj instanceof Integer value) {

        return value + value;
    }

    if (obj instanceof String value) {

        return value + value;
    }
    return null;

}
```

This feature was made permanent in Java 16. But this was not allowed for primitive types, you can use pattern matching only for reference classes like "Integer", "String" or your own custom classes.

Using Java 23, you can now use primitive types in pattern matching for instanceof:

```
Object test(Object obj) {

    if (obj instanceof int value) {
```

```
        return "This is an int";
    }

    if (obj instanceof float value) {

        return "This is a float";
    }
    if(obj instanceof boolean value){

        return "This is a boolean";
    }
    return null;

}
```

Primitive types in instanceof :

Inline, with allowing primitive "type patterns" Java now allows primitive types to be used in instanceof operator as well.

Previously you could only compare reference classes using instanceof operator.

```
if(obj instanceof Integer){

    return "I am an integer";
}
```

Now you can use primitive types like 'int', 'boolean':

```
if(obj instanceof int){
    return "I am a primitive integer";
}
```

Java 23 New Features Simplified

Primitive types in switch:

Until now switch can take byte, short, char, and int values in addition to reference classes objects but not boolean, float, double, or long values.

So. the below code wouldn't compile:

```
switch (user.isLoggedIn()) {
    case true  -> user.id();
    case false -> -1;
}
```

Starting Java 23 you can use these primitive types in switch statements!

There is a limitation though, if you are passing any boolean, float, double or long values then the case statements should contain only the respective primitive type or its wrapper type (ie) Wrapper type of int is Integer)

The below code is invalid:

```
float v = ...
switch (v) {
    case 0 -> 5f;
    case float x when x == 1f -> 6f + x;
    case float x -> 7f + x;
}
```

since the first case statement contains an integer 0.

Changing to 0f will work:

```
float v = ...
switch (v) {
    case 0f -> 5f;
    case float x when x == 1f -> 6f + x;
```

```
    case float x -> 7f + x;
}
```

Casting safeguards:

When you use instanceof operator along with pattern matching for primitive types, the casting is done automatically.

But what if different primitive types are cast to each other.

Like you pass a float but check for the instance of int and do pattern matching, will it work?

It will as long as there is no loss of information!

What information loss am I referring to here?

Consider the below code:

```
int i = 500;

float f = i;

int n = (int)f;

System.out.println(n);
```

The above code prints 500, the original integer value, since the number is small.

But change the value to a very high value and you lose information after the casting.

```
int i = 599999999;

float f = i;

int n = (int)f;

System.out.println(n);
```

The above code prints 600000000 instead of 599999999!

So instanceof operator will return false in that case.

So the same code :

```
if(i instanceof float fl){


}
```

Will return true if i = 500 and return false if i = 599999999 though both are integers!

Here are more examples from open jdk doc:

```
byte b = 42;
b instanceof int;      // true

int i = 42;
i instanceof byte;     // true

int i = 1000;
i instanceof byte;     // false, i is too big to fit into byte

int i = 16_777_217;    // 2^24 + 1
i instanceof float;    // false
```

```
i instanceof double;     // true
i instanceof Integer;    // true
i instanceof Number;     // true

float f = 1000.0f;
f instanceof byte;       // false
f instanceof int;        // true
f instanceof double;     // true

double d = 1000.0d;
d instanceof byte;       // false
d instanceof int;        // true
d instanceof float;      // true

Integer ii = 1000;
ii instanceof int;       // true
ii instanceof float;     // true
ii instanceof double;    // true

Integer ii = 16_777_217;
ii instanceof float;     // false
ii instanceof double;    // true
```

Nested patterns in Records:

Java extended pattern matching to records too (finalized in Java 21).

For example:

```
record Position(int xCoordinate, int yCoordinate) {}
 void printSum(Object obj) {
   if (obj instanceof Position(int xCoordinate, int yCoordinate)) {
     System.out.println(xCoordinate+yCoordinate);
```

```
    }
}
```

Note the instanceof operator, both the field references of Position records are passed as parameters. These are matched through pattern matching automatically and you don't need to explicitly extract the field values from the record.

Now what if you do this:

```
record Position(int xCoordinate, int yCoordinate) {}
if(obj instanceof Position(float xCoordinate, float yCoordinate)){
        System.out.println(xCoordinate+yCoordinate);
}
```

Will the above work?

The record Position has two fields and both are integers.

But while doing instanceof operation we are passing float values above.

What will happen now?

This will work! since Java will automatically cast the above integer values to float AND if there is any loss of information like we saw earlier it will return false instead of true.

So, if you pass the values (100,200) for the x and y coordinates then the above **instanceof** will return true and the sum of the two coordinates get printed but if you pass a very high value (say 599999999) for any of the coordinates the **instanceof** operator will return false (because there is loss of information) and the if loop exits.

Note: This is a preview feature

Module Import Declarations

How do you reuse code in java?

By importing a class or a package or an interface.

```
import java.util.Map;
import java.util.*;
```

In the above example **java util. Map** is an interface and you import it using import keyword. **java. util** is a package and you import it using import keyword and asterisk (*) regular expression.

In Java 9, Java introduced modules.

You can now pack together related packages in a module. But how do you import a module, in other words reuse the code in a module?

You first create a **module – info.java** file. Then you declare the dependent modules of your module inside it.

```
module mymodule{

   requires java.sql;

}
```

In the above example, mymodule has dependency on the code from java.sql module and declares it using requires keyword.

This is not enough. For importing the code in a class in your module, you need to import it using import keyword just like you do it before import java.sql.*;

One more restriction is, you can only import a module inside another module. That is, first you need to declare the dependency **in module info. java** file and then use import statements in your class where you want to import. You cannot import directly without declaring the dependency.

That restriction is removed now.

You can now import a module directly in your class using "'import module" Keyword.

import module java.sql;

When you do so, all the packages and classes will automatically get imported in your class. You don't need to use import keyword to import each class or package separately.

In the above example, all packages under **java.sql module** get imported into your current class along with all the classes under them.

Transitive dependencies

Whenever you import a class or package in your class and the imported class has a dependency on another class, then you have to import the dependent class as well.

Same is the case with packages.

For example if you are using **java.sql.SQLXML** interface you need to import both **java.sql** and **javax.xml.transform** packages since the **SQLXML** interface has a transitive dependency on **java.xml.transform** package.

But using "import module" keyword, when you import a module, the transitive dependencies are imported as well.

For example, if module A has a transitive dependency on module B and you import module A, then both module A and B get imported for you. This works only if the dependency is declared as a transitive dependency using "requires transitive'" B keywords.

Example:

module A{

requires transitive B;

}

In the above case whichever module or class imports module A also gets module B.

But for for the below example:

module A{

  requires B;

}

B is not a transitive dependency. It is a local dependency only specific to module A.

So it will not be imported when you import module A .

When to use import module keyword?

Using "import module" avoids unnecessary import statements.

But sometimes (as a best practice) you need those import statements for better readability. You will know where your dependencies are coming from just looking at the import statements . In those cases, you can avoid using 'import module" statement.

You will need to use it when:

- You are doing local development to test some new feature introduced in Java

- You are doing POC (Proof of Concept) development

- You are prototyping code.

Ambiguous imports

What if you have the same class name in two different packages and they are imported as part of the same module or you import two different modules which has the same class name.

For example,

```
import module java.base;
import module java.sql;
```

Date d = ... // ambiguous

In the above case Date class is present both in **java.base** and **java.sql** modules so the above code won't compile.

You can resolve it by just adding a specific import statement:

```
import module java.base;
import module java.sql;

import java.sql.Date;

Date d = … // ambiguous
```

Note: This is a preview feature

Implicitly Declared Classes and Instance Main Methods

If you are a beginner to Java, learning to just print "Hello World" onto the console can be a daunting and confusing task.

Here is a sample code:

```
public class HelloWorld {
    public static void main(String[] args) {
        System.out.println("Hello, World!");
    }
}
```

What is that public for?

Why do I need a class, what does it mean and why is it needed just to print a text?

What is this static keyword?

What is this String[] ?

Why is it passed as an argument?

I just want to print a text!!

And wait,

What is this System.out.println?

Intimidating!!

A beginner wanting to learn Java may lose interest.

These keywords are helpful only for complex enterprise applications.

- You use class to encapsulate code. This helps in hiding implementation details

- You use public keyword to expose your code to other code written in the same project

- You use static to call a method without creating a new instance

- You use String[] as argument in the main method because the main method is supposed to get an input of an array of strings from the shell command

- You use System.out.println() because println() is a static method belonging to System class

All this knowledge is not required in the beginning when you are starting to learn a new language.

They can be learned progressively.

The guardians of Java have decided to solve this problem!

Going forward all you have to write to say "Hello World" is this:

```
void main() {
   println("Hello, World!");
}
```

Simple as that.

No boiler plate code, no need to understand advanced concepts.

Just copy the paste the above code in a file, name the file with the suffix ".java" and run it!

How does it work internally?

Implicit classes:

Java hasn't changed its core concepts to accommodate the above.

The above code still belongs to a class.

Nothing in Java exists outside a class.

The above code is part of an "implicit" class.

A class without a name.

But this is different from anonymous classes.

You cannot instantiate it, you cannot refer it from other classes.

And it should have a main method.

You can have any number of implicit classes in a project, all with a main method. They will be considered as separate small programs and can be run independently.

Automatic imports:

Java automatically imports the following three static methods in a implicit class:

```
public static void println(Object obj);
public static void print(Object obj);
public static String readln(String prompt);
```

So you don't have to call System.out.println() just println() would do.

All the above three static methods are included in a new package **java.io.IO** package and this package is automatically imported in implicit classes.

In addition **java.base** package is also automatically imported so you can use data structures like "List" as shown in below example:

```
void main() {
    var authors = List.of("James", "Bill", "Guy", "Alex", "Dan", "Gavin");
    for (var name : authors) {
        println(name + ": " + name.length());
    }
}
```

Console interaction:

Until now to read an input from the shell, you need to use the below code:

```
try {
    BufferedReader reader = new BufferedReader(new InputStreamReader(System.in));
    String line = reader.readLine();
    ...
} catch (IOException ioe) {
    ...
}
```

Again a beginner needs to know what a try catch block is ,

Java 23 New Features Simplified

Understand BufferedReader,

Understand InputStreamReader,

Understand System.in,

Understand what IOException is!

Too much boilerplate code just to get a text input from the command line.

All the above can now be replaced by the below code:

```
void main() {
    String name = readln("Please enter your name: ");

    println(name);
}
```

readln() will take care of reading input from the console and this is imported automatically as mentioned earlier .

Easy for a beginner to get some text from the console and print it.

Imagine that tiny sense of achievement!

This will also help senior programmers to develop tiny programs for prototyping or wanting to test a piece of logic.

Note: This feature is in third preview

Flexible Constructor Bodies

Constructors are special functions in Java.

They allow you to create new instances and initialize them:

```java
public class Person{

  String name;
  int age;

    public Person(String name , int age){

      this.name = name;
      this.age = age;
    }
}
```

While doing so they also allow you to call super class constructors using super() method :

```java
public class SportsPerson extends Person {

    String sportsName;

    public SportsPerson(String name, int age, String sportsName){

        super(name,age);
        this.sportsName = sportsName;
```

```
        }
}
```

This way you can initialize common values defined in the super class. You can also call other constructors in the same class using this() keyword.

```java
public class SportsPerson extends Person {

        String sportsName;
        String gender;

        public SportsPerson(String name, int age, String sportsName){

                super(name,age);
                this.sportsName = sportsName;

        }
        public SportsPerson(String name, int age, String sportsName,String
gender){

                this(name,age,sportsName);
                this.gender = gender;

        }
}
```

But Java does not allow to execute any statement before the super() method call or the this() method call.

```java
public class SportsPerson extends Person {

        String sportsName;
        String gender;
```

```java
    public SportsPerson(String name, int age, String sportsName){


        this.sportsName = sportsName; --> NOT ALLOWED!!!
        super(name,age);

    }

    public SportsPerson(String name, int age, String sportsName,String
gender){

        // NOT ALLOWED!!!
        this.gender = gender;

        this(name,age,sportsName);



    }
}
```

Java did this to make sure constructors are executed top down:

Super class constructor first followed by sub class constructor and nothing should get executed in between.

But there are certain use cases where you may need to execute statements before calling the super() constructor.

Validating subclass constructor arguments

Consider doing a validation on one of the constructor arguments:

```java
public class SportsPerson extends Person {

    String sportsName;
```

```
    String gender;

    public SportsPerson(String name, int age, String sportsName){

        //not allowed until now
        if(age < 0 || age > 120) throw new IllegalArgumentException();
        super(name,age);
        this.sportsName = sportsName;

    }

}
```

To achieve this before, you had to implement a work around.

You need to create a helper method and call that as an argument to super() method:

```
public class SportsPerson extends Person {

    String sportsName;
    String gender;

    public SportsPerson(String name, int age, String sportsName){

        super(name,validate(age));
        this.sportsName = sportsName;

    }

    private static int validate(int age){

    if(age < 0 || age > 120) throw new IllegalArgumentException();

        return age;
```

```
        }
    }
```

There is no statement above the super() method call above.

You need to create a separate method which returns the argument value after validating it and then invoke it within the super() method arguments.

Preparing arguments for the superclass

Let's say in the above example before initializing name through the super constructor class you want to append a title to it:

```
public class SportsPerson extends Person {

    String sportsName;
    String gender;

    public SportsPerson(String name, int age, String sportsName){

        super(name,age);
        this.sportsName = sportsName;

    }
    public SportsPerson(String name, int age, String sportsName,String gender){


        //preparing argument for super class constructor
        // not allowed until now
        if(gender.equalsIgnoreCase("Male")){
```

```
            this.name = "Mr "+name;
        }else{
            this.name = "Mrs "+name;
        }
        this(name,age,sportsName);
        this.gender = gender;


    }
}
```

The above two code is valid starting Java 22 (as a preview feature)

You can execute statements before the super() and this() method calls.

But there are limitations.

Referencing current instance

You cannot read the current instance or invoke methods using it before the super() and this() calls:

```
class Person{

    int age;

    Person() {

        System.out.print(this);  // Error - refers to the current instance

        var x = this.age;        // Error - explicitly refers to field of the current
instance
        this.hashCode();         // Error - explicitly refers to method of the
current instance

        var x = age;             // Error - implicitly refers to field of the current
```

instance
    hashCode();   // Error – implicitly refers to method of the
current instance

    super();// super invoked here

  }

}

Same applies for super keyword as well.

You cannot refer super class variables and call super class constructor before invoking super() or this() methods.

BUT

You can assign values to the fields of the current instance before calling super() or this().

The following is valid:

```
public class SportsPerson extends Person {

    String sportsName;

    public SportsPerson(String name, int age, String sportsName){


        this.sportsName = sportsName; //this is valid
        super.name = name; //NOT VALID.
        super(name,age);
```

```
    }
}
```

But you cannot assign values to the fields of the super class.

Why would you be allowed to change an object (the current instance) but not read it before it is constructed?

The purpose of a constructor is to construct a valid instance of an object.

Super class is constructed first.

And then the sub class is constructed next.

This order should be followed because the sub class could be referring to the values constructed in the super class.

If you read an object / field of the object before it is constructed, you are reading an invalid state of the object.

If you write before constructing it though, by the time the object is constructed fully (by calling super class constructor first and then child constructor) you will have the consistent updated value.

Hence it makes sense to update the fields of an object before it is constructed than to read them.

And again, note that you can only change the values of the current instance and not the super class values.

Note: This feature is in second preview

Class File API

Java isn't perfect for developing web applications.

Hence you need to use some framework like Spring, Hibernate, Quarkus etc.

How do these frameworks insert logic into the code you have already written?

By manipulating class files.

And one of the popular ways to modify class files is to use third party libraries like ASM. Java ships with a version of ASM too (which is a bytecode manipulation and analysis library).

This has a disadvantage:

Java has been making changes to its core library every 6 months now. And with every change it needs to keep the ASM library updated too. ASM belongs to a third party and Java doesn't have much control over it. Also, ASM is cumbersome to use. It would be better if Java has its own class file manipulation API.

And that is exactly what is done in Java 23.

Now you can manipulate compiled Java class files using Java's own Class File API. The classes of the API are added in **java.lang.classfile** package and its sub packages.

The components of Class File API

Class file API contains mainly three components:

1. Element

2. Builder

3. Transform

Element

Element represents some part of a class: a field, a method, an instruction or the whole class file itself.

Builder

A builder is used to build elements.

Transform

A Transform takes an element and a builder and takes care of transforming the element into other elements.

Examples:

Creating a new method

Let's see an example of how to use Class File API.

Let's say you want to generate the following method in a class (example from openjdk docs):

```
void fooBar(boolean z, int x) {
    if (z)
```

```
    foo(x);
  else
    bar(x);
}
```

With ASM you need to use visitor pattern and the code looks like this:

```
ClassWriter classWriter = ...;
MethodVisitor mv = classWriter.visitMethod(0, "fooBar", "(ZI)V", null, null);
mv.visitCode();
mv.visitVarInsn(ILOAD, 1);
Label label1 = new Label();
mv.visitJumpInsn(IFEQ, label1);
mv.visitVarInsn(ALOAD, 0);
mv.visitVarInsn(ILOAD, 2);
mv.visitMethodInsn(INVOKEVIRTUAL, "Foo", "foo", "(I)V", false);
Label label2 = new Label();
mv.visitJumpInsn(GOTO, label2);
mv.visitLabel(label1);
mv.visitVarInsn(ALOAD, 0);
mv.visitVarInsn(ILOAD, 2);
mv.visitMethodInsn(INVOKEVIRTUAL, "Foo", "bar", "(I)V", false);
mv.visitLabel(label2);
mv.visitInsn(RETURN);
mv.visitEnd();
```

With Class File API you use builder pattern:

```
CodeBuilder classBuilder = ...;

classBuilder.withMethod("fooBar", MethodTypeDesc.of(CD_void,
CD_boolean, CD_int), flags,
            methodBuilder -> methodBuilder.withCode(codeBuilder -> {
  codeBuilder.iload(codeBuilder.parameterSlot(0))
       .ifThenElse(
```

```
            b1 -> b1.aload(codeBuilder.receiverSlot())
                .iload(codeBuilder.parameterSlot(1))
                .invokevirtual(ClassDesc.of("Foo"), "foo",
                        MethodTypeDesc.of(CD_void, CD_int)),
            b2 -> b2.aload(codeBuilder.receiverSlot())
                .iload(codeBuilder.parameterSlot(1))
                .invokevirtual(ClassDesc.of("Foo"), "bar",
                        MethodTypeDesc.of(CD_void, CD_int))
        .return_();
});
```

Class File API uses lambda extensively which allows Java to do optimizations internally while generating the final code.

Let's take another example.

Remove a method

We want to remove methods starting with the name "debug".

The code in Class File API would be:

```
ClassFile cf = ClassFile.of();
ClassModel classModel = cf.parse(bytes);
byte[] newBytes = cf.build(classModel.thisClass().asSymbol(),
    classBuilder -> {
        for (ClassElement ce : classModel) {
            if (!(ce instanceof MethodModel mm
                && mm.methodName().stringValue().startsWith("debug"))) {
                classBuilder.with(ce);
            }
        }
    });
```

Swap invocation of method from one class to another

Let's say you want to swap the invocation of methods on class Foo to class Bar:

```
CodeTransform codeTransform = (codeBuilder, e) -> {
   switch (e) {
      case InvokeInstruction i when
i.owner().asInternalName().equals("Foo") ->
         codeBuilder.invoke(i.opcode(), ClassDesc.of("Bar"),
                            i.name().stringValue(),
                            i.typeSymbol(), i.isInterface());
      default -> codeBuilder.accept(e);
   }
};
MethodTransform methodTransform =
MethodTransform.transformingCode(codeTransform);
ClassTransform classTransform =
ClassTransform.transformingMethods(methodTransform);
ClassFile cf = ClassFile.of();
byte[] newBytes = cf.transform(cf.parse(bytes), classTransform);
```

The API though tough to read for a developer who doesn't deal with manipulating class files, will be relatively easier to read for one who works on frameworks.

Framework creators need no longer worry about the version incompatibility of code generation tools like ASM while manipulating Java class files.

This will reduce the time of shipping framework features to production.

Note: This feature is in second preview in Java 23.

Vector API

Let us say you want to add the elements of two arrays which are of equal size.

The first element of array 1 should be added to the first element of array 2,

The second element of array 1 to the second element of array 2 and so on until you reach the end of the arrays.

How do you do this in Java?

Using a code like this:

```
public class ScalarExample {
    public static void main(String[] args) {
        int[] arr1 = {1, 2, 3, 4, 5};
        int[] arr2 = {6, 7, 8, 9, 10};
        int[] result = new int[5];

        for (int i = 0; i < arr1.length; i++) {
            result[i] = arr1[i] + arr2[i];
        }

        // Print result
        for (int value : result) {
            System.out.print(value + " ");
        }
    }
}
```

Pretty straightforward!

There is something to note here which is very obvious. You perform one addition at a time. So, in the above case since the array size is 5 you perform 5 operations sequentially through 5 CPU instructions.

This is called a scalar operation.

What if you could do this addition in a single CPU instruction and the 5 elements are added at the same time?

That can be done using Vector Computation.

Java is experimenting with this using a Vector API which is in the incubation phase now and once stable will be brought into JDK as a preview feature and finally accepted as a permanent feature.

Vector Computation and How it Works?

Here is an example for a Vector computation on two arrays:

```java
import jdk.incubator.vector.*;

public class VectorExample {
    public static void main(String[] args) {
        int[] arr1 = {1, 2, 3, 4, 5, 6, 7, 8, 9, 10};  // Length 10
        int[] arr2 = {6, 7, 8, 9, 10, 11, 12, 13, 14, 15};  // Length 10
        int[] result = new int[10];  // Result array of length 10

        // Create a vector for each array (assuming the vector size is 256 bits)
        VectorSpecies<Integer> SPECIES = IntVector.SPECIES_256;

        // Process in chunks of 8 (as that is the vector's capacity)
        int i = 0;
        for (; i <= arr1.length - SPECIES.length(); i += SPECIES.length()) {
```

```
        // Load 8 elements from each array into vectors
        IntVector v1 = IntVector.fromArray(SPECIES, arr1, i);
        IntVector v2 = IntVector.fromArray(SPECIES, arr2, i);

        // Add the vectors together element-wise
        IntVector sum = v1.add(v2);

        // Store the result back into the result array
        sum.intoArray(result, i);
    }

    // Process the remaining elements (less than a full vector)
    for (; i < arr1.length; i++) {
        result[i] = arr1[i] + arr2[i];
    }

    // Print result
    for (int value : result) {
        System.out.print(value + " ");
    }
  }
}
```

Let's drill into the code.

You first create a Vector species:

VectorSpecies<Integer> SPECIES = IntVector.SPECIES_256;

This is the size of the vector.

In the above case the species size is 256 bits and holds Integer type which means it can hold 8 integer values (32 bits for one Integer).

So, at a time 8 integers can be added simultaneously!

Imagine an 8x performance improvement for a really large array of size say a billion integers!

It won't be 8x exactly as there will be overhead in using a Vector API but still the performance will be much faster compared to a regular Scalar computation.

Once you define the species, you iterate using a for loop 8 integers at a time:

for (; i <= arr1.length - SPECIES.length(); i += SPECIES.length()) {

The upper bound in the for loop is **arr1.length—SPECIES.length()** instead of **arr1.length** so that if the array length is not a multiple of 8, you don't enter the for loop for the left over elements.

And then you create vectors of size 8 from each array:

IntVector v1 = IntVector.fromArray(SPECIES, arr1, i);
IntVector v2 = IntVector.fromArray(SPECIES, arr2, i);

You create a vector using **fromArray** method which takes the Vector SPECIES instance as the first argument, the array as the second argument and the index into the array as the third argument.

Then you add the two vectors:

IntVector sum = v1.add(v2);

The above operation is performed as a single instruction on 16 integers (8 from each array) instead of 8 different addition instructions.

This is called SIMD (Single Instruction Multiple Data)

And for the above to work you need CPUs which support SIMD instructions.

Most modern CPUs come with SIMD but if they don't, the entire Vector API adds no value! (the instructions will still work, and you will get the output though)

Finally, you convert the result vector to an integer array:

sum.intoArray(result, i);

There is one more step.

Since the vector takes 8 integers at a time, if the array size is not a multiple of 8 then there will be left over elements.

You add them separately using a scalar operation (the number of left over elements is less than 8 , a very small number and hence won't impact the performance)

```
for (; i < arr1.length; i++) {
        result[i] = arr1[i] + arr2[i];
 }
```

In case if you don't want to do the scalar computation at the end, you can do it using the below code:

```
import jdk.incubator.vector.*;

public class VectorExample {
   public static void main(String[] args) {
       int[] arr1 = {1, 2, 3, 4, 5, 6, 7, 8, 9, 10}; // Length 10
       int[] arr2 = {6, 7, 8, 9, 10, 11, 12, 13, 14, 15}; // Length 10
       int[] result = new int[10]; // Result array of length 10
```

```
    // Create a vector for each array (assuming the vector size is 256
bits)
    VectorSpecies<Integer> SPECIES = IntVector.SPECIES_256;

    // Process in chunks of 8 (as that is the vector's capacity)
    int i = 0;
    for (; i <= arr1.length; i += SPECIES.length()) {

        var mask = SPECIES.indexInRange(i, arr1.length);
        // Load 8 elements from each array into vectors
        IntVector v1 = IntVector.fromArray(SPECIES, arr1, mask);
        IntVector v2 = IntVector.fromArray(SPECIES, arr2, mask);

        // Add the vectors together element-wise
        IntVector sum = v1.add(v2);

        // Store the result back into the result array
        sum.intoArray(result, i);
    }


    // Print result
    for (int value : result) {
        System.out.print(value + " ");
    }
  }
}
```

In the above code there are a few changes:

- the for loop upper bound is **arr1.length** instead of **arr1.length — SPECIES.length()** as we want to go inside the for loop for the left-over elements

- we have added the below line of code:

var mask = SPECIES.indexInRange(i, arr1.length);

This creates a mask and this is passed over the fromArray() method as an additional argument to make sure the method doesnt break if the number of integers is less than 8:

IntVector v1 = IntVector.fromArray(SPECIES, arr1, mask);
IntVector v2 = IntVector.fromArray(SPECIES, arr2, mask);

But there is a caveat here.

The above code works only in platforms which support "predicate registers" (a register which holds boolean values true and false).

For other machines, you need to go with the former approach.

Use cases

Vector API will be very handy in vector computations like matrix multiplications, arithmetic operations over arrays of huge size, scientific computing and image processing etc.

Note: Vector API is in eighth incubator mode.

Stream Gatherers

Java introduced Stream API in Java 8 release.

This helps to process a stream of values very efficiently either sequentially or in parallel.

Prior to Stream API you had to iterate through a collection of data using for loop and add more logic inside the for loop and also use variables to store temporary values. Stream API simplified the process using builder style API.

It contains three parts:

1. A source (the source of data)

2. Intermediate operations (you do filtering, sorting etc)

3. Terminal operation (this is the final operation which collects the data)

For example:

```
Stream.of(5,6,2,4,67,23) //source
.filter( a -> a < 10) //intermediate operation
.toList(); //terminal operation
```

In the above code,

the first line represents the source of data, the second line represents the intermediate operation (in this case we filter out all the numbers which are less than 10) and finally the third line represents the terminal operation which collects the data into a list.

Note that until the terminal operation is called the above code is not evaluated, meaning the filter operation is not executed until toList() method is called. This is called lazy evaluation and it allows Java to do internal optimizations on the intermediate operations.

There are a lot of useful intermediate operations in Stream API: filter(), sorted(), map(), flatMap(), skip() etc.

But if you want to create your own custom intermediate operation there was no option until now.

For example, let's say you are receiving a stream of alternating stock values, the first number represents the buy value of the stock and the second number represents the sell value of the stock and so on:

[1,4,6,9,2,6,7,10...]

You want to calculate the total profit.

You may write a similar logic as below:

```
var stockValues = Stream.of(1,4,6,9,2,6,7,10).toList();

    int totalProfit = 0;
    for(int i=0;i<stockValues.size();i = i+2){


        int buyValue = stockValues.get(i);
        int sellValue = stockValues.get(i+1);

        int netProfit = sellValue - buyValue;

        totalProfit = totalProfit + netProfit;
```

```
}
System.out.println(totalProfit);
```

In the above code you are collecting all the data from the list first using the terminal operation toList().

So, there is no lazy evaluation here.

Second, you iterate through the data the second time again to perform the logic to find the total profit.

Third, you are creating new temporary variables.

Fourth, the number of lines of code is more compared to using a Stream API.

All these could be avoided if there were an intermediate operation which we could be fired on the stream of data.

There is one other alternative.

You can perform the above logic in the terminal operation (also called Collector operations since they implement Collector interface). But they are also not lazily evaluated and the logic is quite complex to write and hence difficult to maintain.

For example,

Let's say you want to group a collection of ordered elements into fixed size groups of size 3:

Input: [1,24,36,49,52,66,77,80,92]
Output: [[1,24,36] , [49,52,66] ,[77,80,92]]

Using Collectors you can write the below code:

```
var result
      = Stream.of(1,4,6,9,2,6,7,10,12)

      .collect(Collector.of(
         () -> new ArrayList<ArrayList<Integer>>(),
         (groups, element) -> {
            if (groups.isEmpty() || groups.getLast().size() == 3) {
               var current = new ArrayList<Integer>();
               current.add(element);
               groups.addLast(current);
            } else {
               groups.getLast().add(element);
            }
         },
         (left, right) -> {
            throw new UnsupportedOperationException("Cannot be
parallelized");
         }
      ));
```

Though the above approach is correct, there are few shortcomings in the above approach:

One: the above operation is not lazily evaluated,

Two : Since the above operation works on sorted data , you cannot execute them in parallel and need to indicate it by throwing exception like in the above code.

Third: If you want to stop processing after a fixed number of groups you cannot do it since a terminal operation requires all the data to be processed.

An intermediate operation can solve the above issues.

The code could like this if we had an intermediate operation named "windowFixed()"

```
var result = Stream.of(11,22,35,43,57,66,77,89,99)
        .windowFixed(3)
        .toList();
```

Looks very neat!

windowFixed was not available until now.

But what if we could create one?

You can also limit the processing after finding 2 groups using the below code:

```
var result = Stream.of(11,22,35,43,57,66,77,89,99)
        .windowFixed(3)
        .limit(2)
        .toList();
```

limit() is an existing intermediate operation and the above code will stop processing the stream once 2 windows are created, unlike using collectors where the entire stream is processed.

The above code is now possible thanks to Gatherers.

Gatherers

You can now create custom intermediate operations using Gatherers interface.

A gatherer consists of four parts:

1. Initializer

2. Integrator

3. Combiner

4. Finisher

Initializer

An initializer is used to save state of the stream.

For example, you can store the current element in the initializer so that when the next element in the stream is processed you could compare it will the current element.

Integrator

An integrator processes the current element.

You can do your core logic here. You can also stop processing more elements if some condition is reached (let's say you reached the maximum integer value and so don't won't to process the stream anymore)

Combiner

Combiner is applicable only if you want to process the stream in parallel.

Finisher

The finisher is invoked when no more elements are need to be processed.

This is the final step.

Let's create a gatherer for calculating the total profit of stock values earlier mentioned.

Here is the code for the gatherer.

```java
import java.time.Instant;
import java.util.List;
import java.util.ArrayList;
import java.util.stream.Gatherer;


public class Stock {
    static  Gatherer<Integer,?,Integer> profit(){

        class State{
            int total;
            int buyValue;
            boolean isSell;

        }
        return Gatherer.ofSequential(
            State::new
            ,
            Gatherer.Integrator.of((state,input,downstream)->{

                if(!state.isSell){
                    state.buyValue = input;
                    state.isSell = true;
                }else{
                    state.total = state.total + (input -state.buyValue);
                    state.isSell = false;
                }
                    return true;
```

```
        }),
        (state,downstream) ->{

            downstream.push(state.total);
        }
    );
  }
}
```

I have created a gatherer named profit() in the above code. It is created as a static method so that you don't have to create an instance to invoke it.

The method returns a Gatherer of type

Gatherer<Integer,?,Integer>

The first argument represents the input type (in our example it is an Integer) , the second argument represents the state (we mark it as an unknown type in our case using a question mark since we won't be dealing with it explicitly), the third argument represents the output type (which is also an integer in our case)

I have created an inner class State to store the state, mainly two values:

- the buy value of a stock so that it can be referred when the next element (sell value) is processed to calculate the profit.

- the total profit calculated so far

I have also used a boolean flag to know if I need to execute the logic to calculate the profit (if it is a sell value) or just store the buy value (if it is a buy value).

Here is the class:

class State{

    int total;
    int buyValue;
    boolean isSell;

}

Next, we create a sequential gatherer since we are not dealing with parallel execution in our example:

return Gatherer.ofSequential();

Four parameters are passed to the above gatherer:

1. **Initializer:**

State::new

This creates a new instance of State class which can be used to store the state.

2. The integrator:

Here is where the logic to process the current element and store the state is executed.

```
Gatherer.Integrator.of((state,input,downstream)->{

        if(!state.isSell){
           state.buyValue = input;
           state.isSell = true;
        }else{
```

```
                    state.total = state.total + (input -state.buyValue);
                    state.isSell = false;

        }
            return true;
    }),
```

If it is sell value then we calculate the profit and store it.

If it is buy value then we just store the buy value.

3. Combiner

Since this is used only for parallel execution, we don't pass anything here.

4. Finisher

Here we push the final value to downstream:

```
  (state,downstream) ->{

            downstream.push(state.total);
        }
```

Once created we can call the gatherer by passing it as a parameter to gather() method on the stream as below to find the total profit:

```
import java.time.Instant;
import java.util.List;
import java.util.Map;
import java.util.HashMap;
import java.util.stream.Collector;
import java.util.stream.Collectors;
```

```java
import java.util.stream.Stream;

public class Main {
    public static void main(String[] args) {

        var profit =
Stream.of(1,4,6,9,2,6,7,10).gather(Stock.profit()).findAny().get();
        System.out.println(profit);

    }

}
```

Much shorter client code!

We created a gatherer inside a function in the above example.

You can also create a gatherer by implementing Gatherer interface and overriding each of the initializer, integrator, combiner and finisher methods.

Here is how windowFixed gatherer could be written by implementing Gatherer interface (from openjdk docs):

```java
record WindowFixed<TR>(int windowSize)
    implements Gatherer<TR, ArrayList<TR>, List<TR>>
{

    public WindowFixed {
        // Validate input
        if (windowSize < 1)
            throw new IllegalArgumentException("window size must be
positive");
    }
```

```
@Override
public Supplier<ArrayList<TR>> initializer() {
    // Create an ArrayList to hold the current open window
    return () -> new ArrayList<>(windowSize);
}

@Override
public Integrator<ArrayList<TR>, TR, List<TR>> integrator() {
    // The integrator is invoked for each element consumed
    return Gatherer.Integrator.ofGreedy((window, element, downstream)
-> {

        // Add the element to the current open window
        window.add(element);

        // Until we reach our desired window size,
        // return true to signal that more elements are desired
        if (window.size() < windowSize)
            return true;

        // When the window is full, close it by creating a copy
        var result = new ArrayList<TR>(window);

        // Clear the window so the next can be started
        window.clear();

        // Send the closed window downstream
        return downstream.push(result);

    });
}

// The combiner is omitted since this operation is intrinsically
```

```
sequential,
  // and thus cannot be parallelized

  @Override
  public BiConsumer<ArrayList<TR>, Downstream<? super List<TR>>>
finisher() {
    // The finisher runs when there are no more elements to pass from
    // the upstream
    return (window, downstream) -> {
      // If the downstream still accepts more elements and the current
      // open window is non-empty, then send a copy of it downstream
      if(!downstream.isRejecting() && !window.isEmpty()) {
        downstream.push(new ArrayList<TR>(window));
        window.clear();
      }
    };
  }
}
```

In built Gatherers

Java also provides the following inbuilt gatherers

windowFixed, windowSliding, fold, scan and mapConcurrent

windowFixed

We already saw the use case for windowFixed. It groups the input into fixed size windows.

Here is another sample:

```
// output : [[1, 2, 3], [4, 5, 6], [7, 8]]
List<List<Integer>> windows =
    Stream.of(1,2,3,4,5,6,7,8).gather(Gatherers.windowFixed(3)).toList();
```

windowSliding:

windowSliding slides through the input. So if window size is 3 it first groups the first 3 elements, then again starts from second element and takes 3 elements and so on.

Here are few examples:

```
// Output : [[1, 2], [2, 3], [3, 4], [4, 5], [5, 6], [6, 7], [7, 8]]
List<List<Integer>> windows2 =
    Stream.of(1,2,3,4,5,6,7,8).gather(Gatherers.windowSliding(2)).toList();

// Output: [[1, 2, 3, 4, 5, 6], [2, 3, 4, 5, 6, 7], [3, 4, 5, 6, 7, 8]]
List<List<Integer>> windows6 =
    Stream.of(1,2,3,4,5,6,7,8).gather(Gatherers.windowSliding(6)).toList();
```

fold:

Fold will reduce the input according the given logic:

Example:

```
//Output: "123456789"
Optional<String> numberString =
    Stream.of(1,2,3,4,5,6,7,8,9)
        .gather(
            Gatherers.fold(() -> "", (string, number) -> string + number)
        )
        .findFirst()
        .get();
```

scan:

scan does an incremental accumulation like below:

```
// Output: ["1", "12", "123", "1234", "12345", "123456", "1234567", "12345678",
"123456789"]
List<String> numberStrings =
  Stream.of(1,2,3,4,5,6,7,8,9)
     .gather(
        Gatherers.scan(() -> "", (string, number) -> string + number)
     )
     .toList();
```

mapConcurrent

mapConcurrent executes the configured number of concurrent tasks using virtual threads.

Note: Stream Gatherers is a preview feature and will be finalised in upcoming releases.

Structured Concurrency

Let's say you want to perform a group of tasks in Java.

And all these tasks are part of a single unit of work.

And all these tasks can be executed independently.

How can this be done in Java?

You can execute each task sequentially. So you execute task 1 , then task 2 and so on. Each task is blocking code , so the total time taken to execute all the tasks is the sum of time taken for each task.

How can we optimize this?

The problem statement says these tasks can be executed independently. So, you can execute each task concurrently. And, once all the tasks are completed, you can take their outputs and do the final processing.

How to implement this?

Threads are the basic unit of concurrency in Java.

You can execute each task as part of a single thread. You can use the Executor framework provided by Java. You can create an executor instance using Executor.newCachedThreadPool().And then submit each of your task wrapped with Callable.

There is a limitation with this approach.

Java doesn't consider the separate tasks as part of a single unit of work. So, if one of the tasks fail, the other tasks keep executing, though ideally, we would want to cancel the rest of the tasks.

Let's take a sample.

Let's create two tasks.

Task1 returns an operand and task 2 returns another operand.

You just add these two operands.

Let's introduce some lag in each method to simulate a thread (using Thread.sleep() method)

We will do this operation using the different patterns available in Java.

No Concurrency

```java
public static  void noconcurrency{
  try {
      int first = getFirst();
      int second = getSecond();
      System.out.println("The sum is " + (first + second));
    } catch (Exception e) {
      e.printStackTrace();
    }
}
 private static int getFirst() throws Exception {
    Thread.sleep(Duration.ofSeconds(5));
    System.out.println("Returning 100");
    return 100;
  }
  private static int getSecond() throws Exception {
    Thread.sleep(Duration.ofSeconds(5));
```

```
    System.out.println("Returning 400");
    return 400;
}
```

The above code is sequential.

Since we are sleeping 5 seconds while getting each operand the total time taken for calculating the sum in the above case is 10 seconds!

Now we can optimize this.

getFirst() and getSecond() are independent operations. We don't have to wait for each other. So, let's convert them to concurrent tasks.

Unstructured Concurrency

Until now, the best way to implement concurrency in Java was using Executor framework.

Here you convert the two tasks to Callables and then submit them to the executor

Here is a sample code:

```
private static void unstructuredConcurrency() {
    try (var executor = Executors.newCachedThreadPool()) {
        Future<Integer> firstTask = executor.submit(() -> getFirst());
        Future<Integer> secondTask = executor.submit(() -> getSecond());
        int first = firstTask.get();
        int second = secondTask.get();
        System.out.println("The sum is " + first + second);
    } catch (Exception e) {
```

```
      e.printStackTrace();
   }
}
private static int getFirst() throws Exception {
   Thread.sleep(Duration.ofSeconds(5));
   System.out.println("Returning 100");
   return 100;
}
private static int getSecond() throws Exception {
   Thread.sleep(Duration.ofSeconds(5));
   System.out.println("Returning 400");
   return 400;
}
```

Each task is converted to a Callable statement using lambda expression. They are then submitted to the executor in parallel. The executor returns a Future object for each Callable .You then retrieve the result using Future.get() method on each returned future. And you finally add the result.

Since the methods getFirst() and getSecond() are invoked in parallel , the above code took 5 seconds to run in my machine.

There is a limitation in the above code.

If one of the methods fail, the other continues to execute.

Here is an example:

I replaced the getSecond() method with getSecondException() method which throws an exception.getFirst() method is the same.It sleeps for 5 seconds and then prints "Returning 100" returning 100.

```java
private static int getFirst() throws Exception {
    Thread.sleep(Duration.ofSeconds(5));
    System.out.println("Returning 100");
    return 100;
}
private static int getSecondException() throws Exception {
    int a = 5 / 0;
    Thread.sleep(Duration.ofSeconds(5));
    System.out.println("Returning 400");
    return 400;
}
private static void unstructuredConcurrencyException() {
    try (var executor = Executors.newCachedThreadPool()) {

        Future<Integer> firstTask = executor.submit(() -> getFirst());
        Future<Integer> secondTask = executor.submit(() ->
getSecondException());
        int first = firstTask.get();
        int second = secondTask.get();
        System.out.println("The sum is " + first + second);
    } catch (Exception e) {
        e.printStackTrace();
    }
}
```

If you run the above code and notice the output, the getFirst() method gets executed even though getSecondException() method throws error. (The message "Returning 100" gets printed after 5 seconds though the error is thrown before that)

Now let's replace the above code with Structured Concurrency.

Structured Concurrency

Structured Concurrency treats all the independent tasks of a single unit of work as part of the work.

So, if any of the tasks fail it cancels the remaining tasks.

So in the above case getFirst() method will get cancelled out before printing the message since getSecondException().

Here is the code for structured concurrency for the positive flow:

```
private static void structuredConcurrency() {
    try (var scope = new StructuredTaskScope.ShutdownOnFailure()) {
        Supplier<Integer> firstTask = scope.fork(() -> getFirst());
        Supplier<Integer> secondTask = scope.fork(() -> getSecond());
        scope.join().throwIfFailed();
        int first = firstTask.get();
        int second = secondTask.get();
        int sum = first + second;
        System.out.println("The sum is :" + sum);
    } catch (Exception e) {
        e.printStackTrace();
    }
}
```

Notice the class "StructuredTaskScope".

This is the backbone of Structured Concurrency.

You first create a new scope by creating an instance of this class. In the above example we create the instance using the factory method StructuredTaskScope.ShutdownOnFailure(). This makes sure all the tasks are shut down immediately if any of the tasks or even if the parent task (in the above case the parent task is the entire block of code within try catch statement) fail .

Instead of submitting to an executor service, in the above case you create a callable for the task and submit it to scope.fork() method. You fork a new task for the given scope. This method returns a Supplier instead of a Future object. When you do this the tasks start getting executed.

And then you do scope.join() which joins the tasks within that scope and waits untill all the tasks are completed.

throwIfFailed() method throws exception if any of the tasks fail and shuts down the remaining tasks.

Finally you get the output of each task using Supplier.get() method.

This method is non-blocking (You immediately get the output).Both the tasks would have already got completed while calling scope.join() method(which is blocking).

Java doesn't return a Future object here like it does for unstructured concurrency as its purpose is more suitable for the former (Future.get() method is a blocking call etc).

Now let's see how error cases are handled in Structured Concurrency.

Structured Concurrency — Error scenario

Now let's use Structured Concurrency for the error scenario we discussed before.

Let us replace getSecond() method with getSecondException() which throws an exception immediately.

Here is the code:

```
private static void structuredConcurrencyException() {
    try (var scope = new StructuredTaskScope.ShutdownOnFailure()) {
        Supplier<Integer> firstTask = scope.fork(() -> getFirst());
        Supplier<Integer> secondTask = scope.fork(() ->
getSecondException());
        scope.join().throwIfFailed();
        int first = firstTask.get();
        int second = secondTask.get();
        int sum = first + second;
        System.out.println("The sum is :" + sum);
    } catch (Exception e) {
        e.printStackTrace();
    }
}
```

If you run the above code and notice the output, getFirst() is not printed in this case as it gets cancelled immediately after getSecondException() throws an exception.

This saves time and prevents unnecessary execution of code.

You may not always want to wait until all tasks complete successfully. In some cases, you may want to shut down as soon as any one of the tasks complete successfully.

Let's see it in the next section.

Structured Concurrency — Return on success of a single task

Let's say you have a collection of services. And you want the result from any one of them. As soon as you get one you can quit the remaining calls.

You can do that using StructuredTaskScope.ShutdownOnSuccess() method.

Here is a sample code:

```
private static void structuredConcurrencySuccess() {
    try (var scope = new StructuredTaskScope.ShutdownOnSuccess<>()) {
        scope.fork(() -> getFirst());
        scope.fork(() -> getSecondSlower());
        int result = (int) scope.join().result();
        System.out.println("The result is :" + result);
    } catch (Exception e) {
        e.printStackTrace();
    }
}
private static int getSecondSlower() throws Exception {
    Thread.sleep(Duration.ofSeconds(6));
    System.out.println("Returning 400");
    return 400;
}
```

As you notice in the above code, instead of getSecond() method getSecondSlower() method is invoked which is one second slower. And we are not using Supplier.get() method to get the result. The scope.join() method directly returns the result in the case.

When you run the code, as expected, getFirst() completes first and immediately the result is returned.

You can also specify a deadline within which all the tasks should get completed.

Let's see it in the next section.

Structured Concurrency — With Deadline

In structured concurrency you can specify a deadline within which all the tasks should get completed.

Here is an example:

```
private static void structuredConcurrencyDeadline() {
    try (var scope = new StructuredTaskScope.ShutdownOnFailure()) {
        Supplier<Integer> firstTask = scope.fork(() -> getFirst());
        Supplier<Integer> secondTask = scope.fork(() -> getSecondSlower());
        scope.joinUntil(Instant.now().plusSeconds(5)).throwIfFailed();
        int first = firstTask.get();
        int second = secondTask.get();
        int sum = first + second;
        System.out.println("The sum is :" + sum);
    } catch (Exception e) {
        e.printStackTrace();
    }
}
```

Notice that there is only one change.

Instead of scope.join() you use scope.joinUntil()And you specify the deadline using Instant object. If the tasks don't get completed within that time an exception is thrown.

The getSecondSlower() method takes more than 5 seconds in the above example, so an exception is thrown when the above code is run.

We saw two patterns in Structured Concurrency.

One cancels all the tasks if any one of the tasks fail (ShutdownOnFailure)

Another returns immediately if any of the tasks succeed and cancels all other tasks (ShutdownOnSuccess)

You can write your custom scope by extending StructuredTaskScope. You may ignore partial failures if you want.

Here is the consolidated code for all the use cases discussed above:

```
import java.time.Duration;
import java.time.Instant;
import java.util.concurrent.Executors;
import java.util.concurrent.Future;
import java.util.concurrent.StructuredTaskScope;
import java.util.function.Supplier;
public class App {
  public static void main(String a[]) {
    noconcurrency();
    unstructuredConcurrency();
    unstructuredConcurrencyException();
    structuredConcurrency();
    structuredConcurrencyException();
    structuredConcurrencySuccess();
    structuredConcurrencyDeadline();
  }
  private static void noconcurrency() {
    try {
      long start = System.currentTimeMillis();
      int first = getFirst();
      int second = getSecond();
```

```java
        long end = System.currentTimeMillis();
        System.out.println("The sum is " + (first + second));
        System.out.println("Time taken " + (end - start) / 1000);
    } catch (Exception e) {
        e.printStackTrace();
    }
}
private static void structuredConcurrency() {
    try (var scope = new StructuredTaskScope.ShutdownOnFailure()) {
        Supplier<Integer> firstTask = scope.fork(() -> getFirst());
        Supplier<Integer> secondTask = scope.fork(() -> getSecond());
        scope.join().throwIfFailed();
        int first = firstTask.get();
        int second = secondTask.get();
        int sum = first + second;
        System.out.println("The sum is :" + sum);
    } catch (Exception e) {
        e.printStackTrace();
    }
}
private static void structuredConcurrencyException() {
    try (var scope = new StructuredTaskScope.ShutdownOnFailure()) {
        Supplier<Integer> firstTask = scope.fork(() -> getFirst());
        Supplier<Integer> secondTask = scope.fork(() ->
getSecondException());
        scope.join().throwIfFailed();
        int first = firstTask.get();
        int second = secondTask.get();
        int sum = first + second;
        System.out.println("The sum is :" + sum);
    } catch (Exception e) {
        e.printStackTrace();
    }
}
```

```
private static void structuredConcurrencyDeadline() {
    try (var scope = new StructuredTaskScope.ShutdownOnFailure()) {
        Supplier<Integer> firstTask = scope.fork(() -> getFirst());
        Supplier<Integer> secondTask = scope.fork(() ->
getSecondSlower());
        scope.joinUntil(Instant.now().plusSeconds(5)).throwIfFailed();
        int first = firstTask.get();
        int second = secondTask.get();
        int sum = first + second;
        System.out.println("The sum is :" + sum);
    } catch (Exception e) {
        e.printStackTrace();
    }
}
private static void structuredConcurrencySuccess() {
    try (var scope = new StructuredTaskScope.ShutdownOnSuccess<>()) {
        scope.fork(() -> getFirst());
        scope.fork(() -> getSecondSlower());
        int result = (int) scope.join().result();
        System.out.println("The result is :" + result);
    } catch (Exception e) {
        e.printStackTrace();
    }
}
private static void unstructuredConcurrency() {
    try (var executor = Executors.newCachedThreadPool()) {
        long start = System.currentTimeMillis();
        Future<Integer> firstTask = executor.submit(() -> getFirst());
        Future<Integer> secondTask = executor.submit(() -> getSecond());
        int first = firstTask.get();
        int second = secondTask.get();
        long end = System.currentTimeMillis();
        System.out.println("Time taken " + (end - start) / 1000);
        System.out.println("The sum is " + first + second);
```

```
    } catch (Exception e) {
        e.printStackTrace();
    }
}
private static void unstructuredConcurrencyException() {
    try (var executor = Executors.newCachedThreadPool()) {
        long start = System.currentTimeMillis();
        Future<Integer> firstTask = executor.submit(() -> getFirst());
        Future<Integer> secondTask = executor.submit(() ->
getSecondException());
        int first = firstTask.get();
        int second = secondTask.get();
        long end = System.currentTimeMillis();
        System.out.println("Time taken " + (end - start) / 1000);
        System.out.println("The sum is " + first + second);
    } catch (Exception e) {
        e.printStackTrace();
    }
}
private static int getFirst() throws Exception {
    Thread.sleep(Duration.ofSeconds(5));
    System.out.println("Returning 100");
    return 100;
}
private static int getSecond() throws Exception {
    Thread.sleep(Duration.ofSeconds(5));
    System.out.println("Returning 400");
    return 400;
}
private static int getSecondException() throws Exception {
    int a = 5 / 0;
    Thread.sleep(Duration.ofSeconds(5));
    System.out.println("Returning 400");
    return 400;
```

```
    }
    private static int getSecondSlower() throws Exception {
        Thread.sleep(Duration.ofSeconds(6));
        System.out.println("Returning 400");
        return 400;
    }
}
```

Note: This feature is in third preview and will be a permanent feature in the next release.

Scoped Values

How do you pass data from one method to another in Java?

Through method parameters.

Let's say method A calls method B which in turn calls method C. And you want some data generated in method A in method C. Though you don't want this data in method B you will still be passing the data as a parameter to method B and then pass it again to method C. This might get cumbersome in certain scenarios.

Is there any way to skip all the intermediate transfer and pass data directly from one method to another which are not directly linked?

There is a way through Thread Variables. It stores variable specific to a thread. So, if method A calls method B which in turn calls method C all part of a single request you can set the data in a thread local variable and use it in any method. Frameworks already use this method.

For example, to store information of the currently logged in user, you could write code like this:

```
class Server {
    final static ThreadLocal<Principal> PRINCIPAL = new ThreadLocal<>();

    void serve(Request request, Response response) {
        var level    = (request.isAuthorized() ? ADMIN : GUEST);
        var principal = new Principal(level);
        PRINCIPAL.set(principal);
        Application.handle(request, response);
    }
}
```

The object PRINCIPAL contains the logged in user details and is set in a thread local variable. You can refer to this variable anywhere in your code, for example if you need it while connecting to the database, you can retrieve it like below:

```
class DBAccess {
  DBConnection open() {
    var principal = Server.PRINCIPAL.get();


      ....

  }
}
```

You just call get() method in the thread local variable.

But thread local variables have few disadvantages:

It is mutable

You can set a thread local variable and then update it later in any part of the code.

You do this using set() method just like you did while creation.

This can lead to confusion particularly because it is not easy to find out where the variable is updated again.

This can also lead to flaws in your code logic when you are expecting a particular value because you set it somewhere but later it got updated to some other value and so you get a different value.

Memory leaks:

Thread Local variables exist in memory as long as the thread lives.

You can manually destroy the variable but developers can often forget to do so.

This can lead to memory leaks.

Expensive inheritance

If you create a thread variable for a particular thread and then create a child thread for that thread, one more copy of the variable is created for the child thread.

If your application generates millions of threads (including parent and child), you will then have millions of copies !

Scoped Values

To resolve the above issues, Java came up with Scoped Values.

It is immutable

Scoped Values unlike thread variables are immutable.

Once created you cannot change its value.

It is destroyed automatically

When you create a scoped variable, you also define its scope.

And the variable gets destroyed once the scope is over.

Child threads share parent thread's copy

Since scoped values are immutable, it makes no sense to create a new copy for the child threads.

So they share the copy of the parent thread.

This saves a lot of memory if you have millions of threads generated.

Now let's see how to create a scoped value.

Let's update the server code with scoped values instead of thread local variables.

```
class Server {
    final static ScopedValue<Principal> PRINCIPAL
        = ScopedValue.newInstance();
```

```
void serve(Request request, Response response) {
    var level   = (request.isAdmin() ? ADMIN : GUEST);
    var principal = new Principal(level);
    ScopedValue.where(PRINCIPAL, principal)
            .run(() -> Application.handle(request, response));
  }
}
```

As you see Scoped Value is declared as a final static variable just like thread local variables.

But they are created using Factory method newInstance()

Then while creating the scoped value you call the where() method and then you set the scope by calling the subsequent code inside run() method.

It follows the below format:

ScopedValue.where().run()

Instead, you can also use the below syntax:

ScopedValue.runWhere()

In this case the previous code needs to be refactored to:

**ScopedValue.runWhere(PRINCIPAL, principal,()->
Application.handle(request, response));**

The PRINCIPAL variable will now be available within the scope of the lambda function passed to run / runWhere method.

Also, it is available further down the method call.

In the above example Application.handle() method is passed as a lambda function.

Application.handle() method in turn can call another method where you can access the scoped value.

That method in turn can call another method where also the scoped value will be accessible.

You can access the variable just like thread local variables:

```
class DBAccess {
  DBConnection open() {
    var principal = Server.PRINCIPAL.get();


    ...
  }
}
```

But what if you want to return a value from the lambda function.

Then you can use call() method instead of run() method.

You can use the below format:

```
ScopedValue.where().call()
```

Or

```
ScopedValue.callWhere()
```

Here is an example:

```
class Server {
  final static ScopedValue<Principal> PRINCIPAL
    = ScopedValue.newInstance();

  void serve(Request request, Response response) {
    var level   = (request.isAdmin() ? ADMIN : GUEST);
    var principal = new Principal(level);
    var returnValue =  ScopedValue.where(PRINCIPAL, principal)
          .call(() -> Application.handle(request, response));
  }
}
```

Rebinding scoped values:

The scoped values are immutable which means you cannot modify its value once it is set. But there may be cases when one of the methods inside the original method needs a different value for the same variable. You can achieve this by creating a new scope as below:

```
private static final ScopedValue<String> X = ScopedValue.newInstance();

void foo() {
    ScopedValue.runWhere(X, "hello", () -> bar());
}

void bar() {
    System.out.println(X.get()); // prints hello
    ScopedValue.runWhere(X, "goodbye", () -> baz());
    System.out.println(X.get()); // prints hello
}

void baz() {
    System.out.println(X.get()); // prints goodbye
}
```

In the above case the value of the scoped variable X is "goodbye" only within the scope created inside the bar() method. Once the scope exits the original value of "hello" is the value of X (even within the bar() method)

Note: Scoped value is in third preview now and will become a permanent feature in the next release.

ZGC: Generational Model by Default

Java deals with objects.

When a java application runs, a lot of objects get created and live in heap memory.

Java's Garbage Collector destroys the unused objects frequently thereby freeing heap memory.

There are different types of Garbage Collectors:

- Serial Garbage Collector

- Parallel Garbage Collector

- G1 Garbage Collector

- Shenandoah Garbage Collector

- Epsilon Garbage Collector

- Z Garbage Collector (the latest one) which further has two types: Generational and Non Generational

But we don't specify it in the code, isn't it?

By default, Java enables a particular type of Garbage Collector.

Before Java 9, Parallel Garbage Collector was the default.

Since Java 9, G1 Garbage Collector has been the default and it remains so.

Why does Java maintain different Garbage Collectors?

Won't it be sufficient if there is a single one?

Different Garbage Collectors serve different purposes.

For example, certain garbage collectors provide high throughput (amount of work done) but also high latency (how fast you get the response — high latency means it takes more time to respond)

And certain GCs does the reverse — low throughput but less latency.

And certain others provide a balance between the two.

Let's take a quick look at the different garbage collectors mentioned earlier:

Serial Garbage Collector

Garbage collection is done in a single thread which is used by the application. So, whenever Garbage Collection happens your application is paused.

It is like a single person cleans a room and asks everyone else to stop whatever they are doing while they clean.

This is not ideal for huge applications, optimal for small single threaded applications.

You can enable Serial GC using the flag -**XX+UseSerialGC**

(java -XX+UseSerialGC)

Parallel Garbage Collector

Garbage collection is done through multiple threads and each thread still pauses the application but the pauses are less compared to Serial GC.

It is like multiple persons are cleaning different parts of the room and asking only people in the part of the room they clean to pause.

This is an improvement over Serial GC and provides high throughput.

You can enable Parallel GC using the flag **-XX+UseParallelGC**

G1 Garbage Collector

This is similar to Parallel Garbage Collector in that it uses multiple threads but cleans the messiest areas first.

It is like multiple persons are cleaning the room and are targeting the messiest areas first.

This also requires pause but is lesser compared to Parallel GC. It provides a better balance between throughput and latency and is the default mode in Java.

This is the default mode and you don't have to explicitly enable it.

Shenandoah Garbage Collector

This is a further improvement over G1 Garbage Collector for specific cases. It is also multi-threaded but removes objects as soon as it scans it unlike G1 Garbage Collector which only marks the objects for removal while scanning and removes them during another phase (STW — Stop the World phase)

It is like multiple persons are cleaning the room and rearranging the furniture as they clean instead of arranging the furniture after cleaning.

Though Shenandoah GC offers better latency than G1 GC, it is not the default GC for various reasons like:

- G1 is more matured and stable whereas Shenandoah is a new kid on the block

- G1 provides better balance between throughput and latency whereas Shenandoah provides better latency but not as good as throughput

- Shenandoah uses more CPU as compared to G1

You can enable it using **-XX+UseShenandoahGC**

Epsilon Garbage Collector

This means no Garbage Collector at all!

There is no cleaning of unused objects and the application itself has to take care of freeing objects.

You can enable it using **-XX+UseEpsilonGC**

Z Garbage Collector

This is the latest and the most efficient one.

This offers better performance than all the others but still not enabled by default but will very likely be enabled in the future.

From the Java docs:

ZGC is designed for low latency and high scalability. It has been available for production use since JDK 15.

ZGC does the majority of its work while application threads are running, pausing those threads only briefly. ZGC's pause times are consistently measured in microseconds; by contrast the pause times of the default garbage collector, G1, range from milliseconds to seconds. ZGC's low pause times are independent of heap size: Workloads can use heap sizes from a few hundred megabytes all the way up to multiple terabytes and still enjoy low pause times.

For many workloads, simply using ZGC is enough to solve all latency problems related to garbage collection. This works well as long as there are sufficient resources (i.e., memory and CPU) available to ensure that ZGC can reclaim memory faster than the concurrently-running application threads consume it.

ZGC achieves much better latency and throughput using techniques like colored pointers.

You can enable it using **-XX:+UseZGC**

Which one should you use?

- **Small app or single-threaded?** → Serial GC

- **Need high performance and throughput?** → Parallel GC

- **Balanced, low-pause GC for most cases?** → G1 GC (default)

- **Large-scale, ultra-low pause times?** → ZGC or Shenandoah

Coming back to ZGC,

ZGC has two different modes:

- Non Generational

- Generational

Non Generational mode doesn't consider the age of objects. It collects all the objects irrespective of age and does Garbage Collection.

Generational mode considers younger objects first since younger objects tend to die earlier compared to older objects thereby improving efficiency.

From the java docs:

ZGC (Non generational mode) currently stores all objects together, regardless of age, so it must collect all objects every time it runs.

*The **weak generational hypothesis** states that young objects tend to die young, while old objects tend to stick around. Thus, collecting young objects requires fewer resources and yields more memory, while collecting old objects requires more resources and yields less memory. We can thus improve the performance of applications that use ZGC by collecting young objects more frequently*

If you use ZGC, by default the Non Generational Mode would be ON until now.

You can enable Generational Mode using a flag like below (earlier to Java 23):

-XX:+UseZGC -XX:+ZGenerational

Java 23 has deprecated this flag **ZGenerational** and enabled Generational Mode by default.

So if you use the flag **-XX+UseZGC** Generational Mode will be activated.

If you use the flag +ZGenerational, Java will issue a warning that the flag has been deprecated.

What if you want to use Non Generational mode?

Ideally you wouldn't want to but if you still want to you can do it by using "-" symbol instead of "+" with the ZGenerational flag like below:

-XX:+UseZGC -XX:-ZGenerational

The Non Generational Mode will be activated in the above case but still Java will issue a warning that the flag ZGenerational is deprecated

MarkDown Documentation Comments

Documentation is an important part of development.

Any other developer wanting to read your code or is going to make changes on it can understand your code better if you have written proper documentation.

Java lets you document your methods and classes using a combination of HTML and JavaDoc tags.

You start with /** and end with **/ .

For example, here is the documentation for hashCode() method of Java:

```
/**
 * Returns a hash code value for the object. This method is
 * supported for the benefit of hash tables such as those provided by
 * {@link java.util.HashMap}.
 * <p>
 * The general contract of {@code hashCode} is:
 * <ul>
 * <li>Whenever it is invoked on the same object more than once during
 *     an execution of a Java application, the {@code hashCode} method
 *     must consistently return the same integer, provided no information
 *     used in {@code equals} comparisons on the object is modified.
 *     This integer need not remain consistent from one execution of an
 *     application to another execution of the same application.
 * <li>If two objects are equal according to the {@link
```

```
*    #equals(Object) equals} method, then calling the {@code
*    hashCode} method on each of the two objects must produce the
*    same integer result.
* <li>It is <em>not</em> required that if two objects are unequal
*    according to the {@link #equals(Object) equals} method, then
*    calling the {@code hashCode} method on each of the two objects
*    must produce distinct integer results.  However, the programmer
*    should be aware that producing distinct integer results for
*    unequal objects may improve the performance of hash tables.
* </ul>
*
* @implSpec
* As far as is reasonably practical, the {@code hashCode} method defined
* by class {@code Object} returns distinct integers for distinct objects.
*
* @return  a hash code value for this object.
* @see     java.lang.Object#equals(java.lang.Object)
* @see     java.lang.System#identityHashCode
*/
```

These are common JavaDoc tags:

- **@param**: Describes a method parameter.

@param paramName description

- **@return**: Describes the return value of a method.

@return description

- **@throws / @exception**: Describes an exception thrown by a method.

@throws ExceptionName description

- **@see**: Refers to another class, method, or resource.

@see ClassName

- **@deprecated**: Marks a method or class as deprecated.

@deprecated description

- **{@link}**: Creates an inline link to another class or method.

{@link ClassName#methodName}

- **@version**: Specifies the version of the class or method.

@version versionNumber

- **@author**: Specifies the author of the class or interface.

@author name

You can also use HTML tags like <p> to denote a paragraph, <ul> to represent a list, <code> to include snippets etc.

Finally, you can run **javadoc** tool to generate the documentation in HTML format.

javadoc -d docFolderName *.java

You can also generate it easily through IDEs like Eclipse and IntelliJ from their respective menus.

For the above hashCode() method documentation you get a HTML page(go to https://docs.oracle.com to find a sample document)

The problem with above documentation style is tags like {@link} and {@code} are less familiar to developers and cumbersome to use.

To resolve such issues Java now supports Markdown syntax which makes it much easier to write documentation now.

From the open jdk docs:

> - ***Markdown*** *is a popular markup language for simple documents that is easy to read, easy to write, and easily transformed into HTML. Documentation comments are typically not complicated structured documents, and for the constructs that typically appear in documentation comments, such as paragraphs, lists, styled text, and links, Markdown provides simpler forms than HTML. For those constructs that Markdown does not directly support, Markdown allows the use of HTML as well.*

Now you just need to use three forward slashes for the documentation and ignore tags like <p>, <ul> (these will be automatically taken care)

For the above hashCode documentation the equivalent Markdown style would be:

```
/// Returns a hash code value for the object. This method is
/// supported for the benefit of hash tables such as those provided by
/// [java.util.HashMap].
///
/// The general contract of `hashCode` is:
///
///   - Whenever it is invoked on the same object more than once during
///     an execution of a Java application, the `hashCode` method
///     must consistently return the same integer, provided no
information
///     used in `equals` comparisons on the object is modified.
///     This integer need not remain consistent from one execution of an
///     application to another execution of the same application.
///   - If two objects are equal according to the
```

///   [equals][#equals(Object)] method, then calling the

///   `hashCode` method on each of the two objects must produce the

///   same integer result.

///   - It is _not_ required that if two objects are unequal

///   according to the [equals][#equals(Object)] method, then

///   calling the `hashCode` method on each of the two objects

///   must produce distinct integer results. However, the programmer

///   should be aware that producing distinct integer results for

///   unequal objects may improve the performance of hash tables.

///

/// @implSpec

/// As far as is reasonably practical, the `hashCode` method defined

/// by class `Object` returns distinct integers for distinct objects.

///

/// @return a hash code value for this object.

/// @see   java.lang.Object#equals(java.lang.Object)

/// @see   java.lang.System#identityHashCode

Here are the key differences:

- No need to use /** and **/ at the beginning and end

- The paragraph tag <p> is not required, a blank line indicates a paragraph break

- Instead of <ul> and <li> you just use bullets "-"

- Instead of <em> you use _

- Instead of {@code} you use back ticks `

- Instead of {@link} to refer to an element declared elsewhere you can use square brackets:

/// – a module [java.base/]

/// – a package [java.util]

/// – a class [String]

/// – a field [String#CASE_INSENSITIVE_ORDER]

/// – a method [String#chars()]'

A link will be generated in the final documentation which when clicked will take you to the referred element.

Javadoc tags like @return, @parameter will remain the same.

Another advantage of using Markdown syntax is that you can include any characters in the comments unlike in the previous style where you cannot use /** characters as they are reserved for indicating the start of the comment.

Deprecate the Memory Access Methods in sun.misc.Unsafe for Removal

Are there any unsafe methods in Java, provided by Java?

Yes, there are!

In **sun.misc.Unsafe** class.

Why would Java create unsafe methods and put them under a class under the same name?

History

The sun.misc.Unsafe class was introduced in 2022 for third party libraries to perform low level operations like direct access of Java's heap memory and off heap memory. These if not used properly can lead to problems like JVM crashes. Not all libraries do necessary checks before using the unsafe methods so Java has decided to deprecate 79 out of 82 methods in the Unsafe class.

Here are a few sample methods in Unsafe class:

Memory Management:

- allocateMemory(long bytes): Allocates a block of memory outside the JVM heap.

- reallocateMemory(long address, long bytes): Reallocates memory to a new size.

- freeMemory(long address): Frees previously allocated memory.

- setMemory(Object o, long offset, long bytes, byte value): Sets a memory block to a specific value.

- copyMemory: Copies memory from one address to another.

Field Access:

- objectFieldOffset(Field field): Retrieves the offset of a field within an object.

- getInt(Object o, long offset): Reads an int value at the specified offset within an object.

- putInt(Object o, long offset, int value): Writes an int value at the specified offset within an object.

CAS (Compare-and-Swap) Operations:

- compareAndSwapInt(Object o, long offset, int expected, int x): Atomically updates an int field if it holds the expected value.

- Similar methods exist for long and object types.

Thread Management:

- park(boolean isAbsolute, long time): Blocks the current thread.

- unpark(Thread thread): Unblocks a thread.

Array Operations:

- arrayBaseOffset(Class<?> arrayClass): Returns the base offset of the first element in an array.

- arrayIndexScale(Class<?> arrayClass): Determines the scaling factor for indexing an array.

Class Loading:

- defineClass: Defines a class programmatically in the JVM.

- ensureClassInitialized(Class<?> c): Ensures that a class is initialized.

These are internal APIs and not officially part of the public API still libraries could use them.

Alternatives

To perform the same operations done by those methods in a more secure way Java has introduced two new methods:

java.lang.invoke.VarHandle — this one is for managing on heap memory

java.lang.foreign.MemorySegment — this one is for managing off heap memory

Example

For example,

The below code to double an integer atomically using unsafe method:

```java
class Foo {

    private static final Unsafe UNSAFE = ...;   // A sun.misc.Unsafe object

    private static final long X_OFFSET;

    static {
      try {
        X_OFFSET =
UNSAFE.objectFieldOffset(Foo.class.getDeclaredField("x"));
      } catch (Exception ex) { throw new AssertionError(ex); }
    }

    private int x;

    public boolean tryToDoubleAtomically() {
      int oldValue = x;
      return UNSAFE.compareAndSwapInt(this, X_OFFSET, oldValue,
```

```
oldValue * 2);
   }

}
```

can be replaced by the below secure code:

```
class Foo {

   private static final VarHandle X_VH;

   static {
     try {
        X_VH = MethodHandles.lookup().findVarHandle(Foo.class, "x",
int.class);
     } catch (Exception ex) { throw new AssertionError(ex); }
   }

   private int x;

   public boolean tryAtomicallyDoubleX() {
     int oldValue = x;
     return X_VH.compareAndSet(this, oldValue, oldValue * 2);
   }

}
```

Methods not yet deprecated

As earlier mentioned, 79 of 82 methods are deprecated leaving behind 3 methods.

pageSize: This is used to access memory page size and will be deprecated and removed in future release. You need to get the page size directly from OS going forward.

---

throwException: This was used in certain methods to wrap checked exceptions in unchecked exceptions like Class::newInstance but those methods themselves are deprecated now. This will be deprecated and removed in future release as well.

allocateInstance: This is used by some serialization libraries for deserialization and is not going to be replaced in the immediate future although will be removed in the long term.

References:

https://openjdk.org/jeps/455

https://openjdk.org/jeps/466

https://openjdk.org/jeps/467

https://openjdk.org/jeps/469

https://openjdk.org/jeps/473

https://openjdk.org/jeps/471

https://openjdk.org/jeps/474

https://openjdk.org/jeps/476

https://openjdk.org/jeps/477

https://openjdk.org/jeps/480

https://openjdk.org/jeps/481

https://openjdk.org/jeps/482